Francis Davenport

Elements of Music

Francis Davenport

Elements of Music

ISBN/EAN: 9783743344204

Manufactured in Europe, USA, Canada, Australia, Japa

Cover: Foto ©Thomas Meinert / pixelio.de

Manufactured and distributed by brebook publishing software
(www.brebook.com)

Francis Davenport

Elements of Music

ELEMENTS

OF

MUSIC

BY

F. DAVENPORT

PROFESSOR OF HARMONY AND COMPOSITION AT THE
ROYAL ACADEMY OF MUSIC

PUBLISHED UNDER THE AUTHORITY OF THE COMMITTEE

OF THE ROYAL ACADEMY OF MUSIC

NEW IMPRESSION

LONGMANS, GREEN, AND CO.
89 PATERNOSTER ROW, LONDON
NEW YORK AND BOMBAY
1899

PREFACE.

THIS book on the Elements of Music is issued by authority of the Committee of Management of the Royal Academy of Music, who commend it to the study of all who enter this Royal and National Institution as pupils, and of all candidates in the Local Examinations of Musical Students who are not in the Academy. Knowledge of the subjects herein treated is imperative in every musician, the lowest as much as the highest; nay, thorough familiarity with this knowledge is the threshold of musicianship, by which alone the mysteries of the art can be entered. Many meritorious books exist wherein the elements of music are explained, but they mostly go beyond the subjects, or treat some of them incompletely. The object here is to direct attention to matters that entirely precede the study of harmony, and, by confining the student's thoughts for the time within this limit, to make such matters the clearer to understand and the easier to remember. The arrangement of the book, and some of the explanations it contains, have points of novelty which may tend to clearness, and need no preliminary description.

A 2

It presents the result of the writer's experience in training elementary classes in the Academy and in examining candidates throughout the country, and it has been inspected and approved by the professional members of the Managing Body.

G. A. MACFARREN,
Chairman and Principal.

ROYAL ACADEMY OF MUSIC :
November 1883.

DEFINITIONS.

Note—a sign used to represent a musical sound, 1.

Pitch—the height or depth of a sound, 9.

Interval—the difference in pitch between two sounds, 32.

Melody—single notes in succession, 74.

Harmony—two or more notes in combination 73.

Modulation—a change of key.

Diatonic—according to the signature, 29, 69, 76 (note 2).

Chromatic—contrary to the signature (indicated by accidentals) without causing modulation, 29, 69, 80.

Enharmonic—(on a keyed instrument) changing the name without altering the pitch. In the case of other instruments and the voice, *enharmonic* is applied to an interval smaller than a chromatic semitone, 30.

Key—a set of notes in relation to one principal note called the Tonic or Key-note, 40.

Scale—the notes of a key ascending or descending in alphabetical order, 41, 72, 73, 74, 80.

N.B.—*Throughout the book the numbers refer to the Sections in the text. Def. refers to the Definitions.*

ELEMENTS OF MUSIC.

CHAPTER I.

LENGTH OF NOTES AND RESTS.

1. A musical sound is represented by a sign called a Note.[1]

As one sound may last a longer or a shorter time than another, it is necessary to have notes of various appearance to express the different lengths of the sounds they represent.

2. The longest note is called a Semibreve,[2] and is written thus:

Other notes are :—

The Minim .	.	.	written	thus	
,, Crotchet	.	.	,,	,,	
,, Quaver	.	.	,,	,,	
,, Semiquaver .	.	,,	,,	
,, Demisemiquaver .	,.	,,	
,, Semidemisemiquaver	,,	,,	

---

[1] Hence the sound itself is called a Note.

[2] To explain how it happens that the longest note is called a half-short, it is necessary to mention that in earliest written music the longest notes were—the Large ⊏⊐ (*maxima*, hence *minima* or minim was the least or shortest note), and the Long ⊏⊐. The Breve, or Short, was a half-Long, or the fourth part of a Large. Perhaps the clumsiness of the shapes may account for their disuse.

[3] The shape and arithmetical relations of the notes have suggested the French and German methods of naming them. The former call them round, white, black, hooked, double-hooked, &c.; and the latter, taking the semibreve as a whole, call them $\frac{1}{2}$, $\frac{1}{4}$, $\frac{1}{8}$, $\frac{1}{16}$, &c., notes respectively. In the United States the latter method has been adopted.

3. The following table shows the relative length of the above notes, each being twice as long as the one that follows, and half as long as the one that goes before it :—

	Semidemi-semiquavers.	Demi-semiquavers.	Semiquavers.	Quavers.	Crotchets.	Minims.	Semibreve.
Semidemi-semiquavers.	64	32	16	8	4	2	
Demi-semiquavers.	32	16	8	4	2		
Semiquavers.	16	8	4	2			
Quavers.	8	4	2				
Crotchets.	4	2					
Minims.	2						
Semibreve.	0						

4. A sound longer than one of the above notes, but not so long as the one next before it, is written in two ways, by means of a Tie or a Dot. The tie (or bind) is written thus :

and causes the sound to last as long as the minim and crotchet together. A dot placed after the minim $\wp$ · has the same effect. Hence a dot adds to a note half its length—that is, the length of the next note. A second dot $\wp$ ·· adds half the length of the dot before it—that is, the length of the next note but one, and so on. More than two dots are seldom used (122).

5. In the following example, dots are placed underneath the notes whose length they add to the first written note :—

from which it will be seen that a dot serves the same purpose as a tie. The effect of the former is always the same (4), but a tie can unite into a continuous sound notes of any

value. Thus : &c.

6. Sound frequently ceases, and there is silence. This is shown by signs called Rests. Length of notes or sound corresponds with length of rests or silence, and each note gives its name to the rest of the same length.

7. Here are the forms of the rests :—

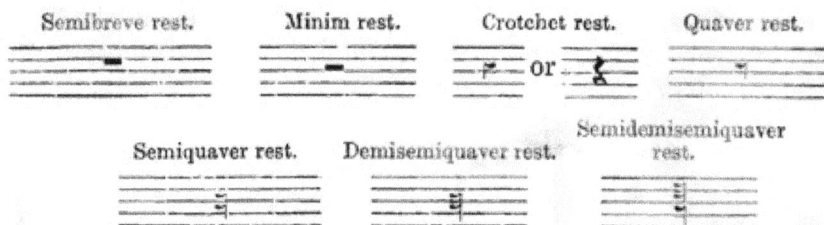

Semibreve rest.	Minim rest.	Crotchet rest.	Quaver rest.

Semiquaver rest.	Demisemiquaver rest.	Semidemisemiquaver rest.

8. Dots placed after rests add to the silence in the same way as they add to the length of notes. Thus :—

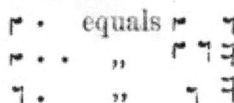

⌐ · equals ⌐ ⌐

⌐ ·· ,, ⌐ ⌐ ⌐

⌐ · ,, ⌐ ⌐

¹ It is obvious that no number of dots can double the length of a note.

CHAPTER II.

PITCH OF NOTES.

9. The height or depth of a sound is called its Pitch.

10. To make this clear to **the eye** in written music, **notes are placed on** five lines and **the spaces between them, called a**

Staff

the height or depth of a sound being **shown by** placing it higher or lower on the staff.[1]

11. When a sound is too high **or too** low to be written on the **staff,** lines are added above **or below for the occasion.**

These have a small, light appearance, **as** compared with the longer five lines, and are therefore called Leger[2] lines :—

&c.[3]

12. Notes thus written **are** said **to be on or above the first,** second, third, &c., leger line over the staff, **and** on or below the first, &c., **leger** line under the staff.

13. The first seven letters of the alphabet, A, B, C, D, E, F, G, are used for the names of the notes,[4] the wide range of

[1] **Five** lines are found most convenient, although **as** many lines and their spaces might be used as there are sounds of different pitch **to** represent. In old music written for the Church, a staff **of four** lines, **or even three,** sufficed for **all the** sounds that were written.

[2] A French word meaning *light.*

[3] The effect of these leger lines **is to** add for **the time additional** lines to the staff. The above **leger** lines could **be** made the **same length as the** five lines of the staff, thus making **a staff of ten lines,** but the **result would be** confusing to the eye.

[4] This **is also the** case in Germany, where, however, B♭ is **called B, and** B♮ is called H (p. **14,** note 1). In France the syllables Ut, Re, Mi, Fa, Sol, La, **are** used, which **are** said to have been taken by Guido Aretino in the eleventh century **from the first** three lines of the following Latin **hymn :—**

musical sounds being expressed by repeated series of these letters.[1]

14. To fix the alphabetical names of notes placed on a staff, a sign called a Clef is used. By this the name of one is fixed, from which the rest may be reckoned.[2]

15. There are three clefs :—

The F clef, written thus : 𝄢 or 𝄢 :

  ,, C   ,,   ,,   ,,   ♮ or ♮

  ,, G   ,,   ,,   ,,   𝄞

16. The C fixed by the C clef is that nearest the middle of the pianoforte keyboard. The F next below and the G next above that C are the notes fixed by the F and G clefs respectively.

17. The F clef is placed on the fourth line of a staff 𝄢

and notes written thereon are for bass (or lowest) voices or instruments. Hence the F clef is called the Bass clef, and the staff is called the Bass staff.

The G clef is placed on the second line of a staff 𝄞

and notes written thereon are for the highest voices or instruments. Hence the G clef is called the Treble [3] clef, and the staff is called the Treble staff.

18. One staff only is required for each voice and the majority of instruments, but some of these contain a wider range of sounds

[1] Ut queant laxis, Resonare fibris,
Mira gestorum Famuli tuorum,
Solve polluti Labii reatum,
Sancte Iohannes.'

The Italians changed Ut into Do for the sake of obtaining a more vocal sound, and Si (taken from the last line of the hymn) was subsequently added.

[1] At one time the letters themselves represented the sounds, capitals being used for one series, small letters for the next, and small letters with one, two, or more lines underneath for the remaining series.

[2] The clef is thus, as its derivation implies, the key to the staff.

[3] See note 1, page 12.

than can be expressed on one staff without the aid of an inconvenient number of leger lines. Hence, for pianoforte music, two staves are used, the higher one for the higher notes, the lower one

for the lower notes :

19. By reckoning upwards from the F or downwards from the G it will be found that the note midway between the two staves is C, which is therefore one leger line below the treble

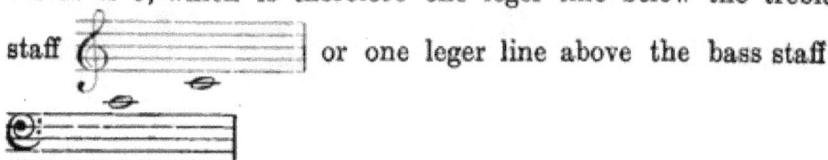

staff   or one leger line above the bass staff

20. If this leger line between the two staves is made equal in length to the lines of the staves, one large staff of eleven lines is formed, which is called the Great Staff. By placing the C clef on this middle line the relative pitch of the three clefs is made

clear: G
         C
         F

21. A staff with the C clef on the first line is called the Soprano staff, on the second the Mezzo-Soprano staff, on the third the Alto, on the fourth the Tenor.[1] Formerly a staff with the F clef on the third line was used for the Baritone voice.

[1] In early music the principal melody was given to the lowest voice but one, hence called tenor because it held or sustained the melody. The lowest voice bore the weight of those above it and was called burden, which expression is retained in the organ pedal stop called bourdon, or bass, which obviously signifies the lowest part. The alto, or high, is next above the tenor and high in relationship to it. The soprano, or highest, is the top part; the mezzo-soprano, or moderately high, next under it. Treble is the third part from the tenor, as the word implies. The alto and tenor are the only staves with the C clef in general use nowadays, the former serving for the viola and alto trombone, the latter for the tenor trombone and the upper notes of the violoncello and bassoon. The treble staff is now generally

Soprano. Mezzo-Soprano. Alto. Tenor. Baritone.

22. To enable the student to observe the difference of pitch implied by these different staves, here are examples of the same notes written on all of them :—

Treble.

G A G E C F F

Soprano.

G A G E C F F

Mezzo-soprano.

G A G E C F F

Alto.

G A G E C F F

Tenor.

G A G E C F F

Baritone.

G A G E C F F

Bass.

G A G E C F F

used for the highest voice, sometimes for the second or alto, and, in printed music, for the tenor voice. It is also used for the violin, flute, hautboy, clarionet, horn, trumpet, the high notes of the viola, and occasionally for the highest notes of the violoncello. Music for the baritone voice is now written on the bass staff. In spite of disuse in England, a clear understanding of the various staves is desirable at least for the professional musician. This is especially the case in acquiring the habit of transposition—*i.e.* playing music in another key than that in which it is written. A melody written in the key of G on the treble staff may thus be transposed into the key of E by imagining the C clef to be on the 1st line, &c.

¹ Thus it will be seen that the same sound which is low on the treble staff is moderately high on the alto and very high on the bass staff. The pitch—namely, the height or depth—of a musical sound is thus picturesquely shown in relation to other sounds on the same staff, while by means of the clef the absolute pitch of each sound is determined in relation to that indicated by the clef. The above examples further show that a note on a line in one staff will be on a line in every staff, and a note once in a space will always be in a space.

23. If notes are now placed on all the lines and spaces of the Great Staff the sounds they represent will be those produced by the corresponding white keys of the pianoforte (see remark p. 12).

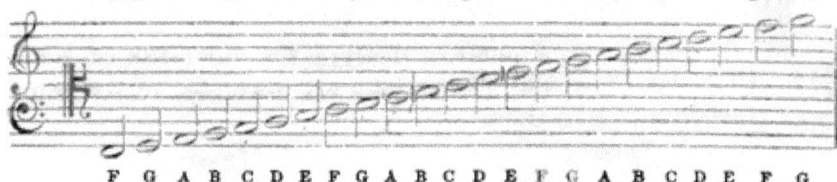

F G A B C D E F G A B C D E F G A B C D E F G

These are called natural notes, as F natural, G natural.

24. The black key *above* any white key has the same alphabetical name, but is represented by a sign called a Sharp, written

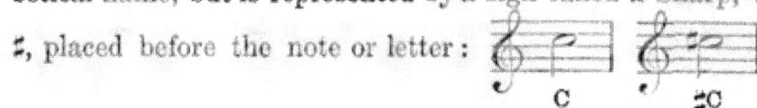

♯, placed before the note or letter:

Similarly, the black note *below* a white note is represented by a sign called a Flat, written ♭[1] placed before the note or letter:

25. The difference in pitch (Def.) between two such sounds is called a Semitone

26. The difference in pitch between any two sounds next to each other in alphabetical order two semitones apart is called a Tone.

27. Let us now write (as on page 15) on the Great Staff the same notes as in 23, using sharps for the intervening sounds ascending, and flats for them descending.

28. Every sound, whether represented by a white or black key on the pianoforte, between the lowest and the highest in the

---

[1] Originally the note *b* was a semitone above A. When B♮ was introduced into music, and when notes instead of letters were employed to indicate the sounds, the letter *b* was employed to signify the ♭ and placed before any note that was to be lowered a chromatic semitone. Hence the sign ♭ is a modification of the letter *b*, and in French the term *bémol* (softened *b*) defines a flat. In Germany the name *b* stands for our B♭, the word *Bé* implies any flat, and the name H is given to our B♮.

F F♭ G G♯ A A♯ &c.

G G♭ F E E♭ D D♭ C &c.

above example, is there represented. There is also a semitone between every two following notes.

29. There are two kinds of semitone. When the two following notes are described by the same letter, the semitone is called chromatic, or minor; when they are described by a different letter it is called diatonic, or major. Thus,

is a chromatic (Def.) semitone

is a diatonic (Def.) semitone.

30. A Double Sharp, written ×, raises a note two semitones; a Double Flat, written ♭♭, lowers a note two semitones. Thus:—

By playing the above notes on the pianoforte, it will be seen that the same key and its sound represents C, ♯B, ♭♭D. Similarly, it will be found that every key, with the exception of the black key between G and A, represents three sounds. Thus:—

C	=	♯B	=	♭♭D		♭F	=	♯E	=	♭G
♯C	=	×B	=	♭D		G	=	×F	=	♭♭A
D	=	×C	=	♭♭E		♯G	=		=	♭A
♯D	=	♭E	=	♭♭F		A	=	×G	=	♭♭B
E	=	×D	=	♭F		♯A	=	♭B	=	♭♭C
F	=	♯E	=	♭♭G		B	=	×A	=	♭C

Each of the three sounds is called the Enharmonic (Def.) of the one next above or below it alphabetically.

31. When a flat or sharp note is followed by the natural note of the same alphabetical name, this sign is used to show the natural, ♮. Thus:—

A note that is double sharp or double flat, followed by the same note sharp or flat, is written thus :—

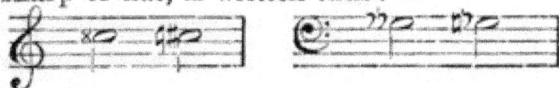

Or more rarely thus :—

CHAPTER III.

INTERVALS.

32. The difference in the pitch of two sounds is called an Interval.

33. Intervals are described by numbers. In counting the numbers the two sounds which are named are included as well as those that come between them.

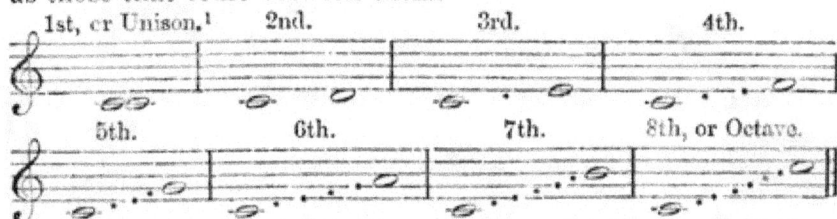

34. An interval within the octave is said to be inverted when the upper note is played an 8ve lower, or the lower note an 8ve higher. The interval thus made is called the Inversion of the original interval.

35. The number of an inverted interval within the octave is found by taking the number of the original interval from nine Thus, the inversion of an Octave or 8th is a 1st or Unison, because 8 from 9 leaves 1. Similarly,

A 7th inverted is a 2nd   A 3rd inverted is a 6th
 ,, 6th   ,,   ,,   3rd   ,, 2nd   ,,   ,,   7th
 ,, 5th   ,,   ,,   4th   ,, 1st   ,,   ,,   8th
 ,, 4th   ,,   ,,   5th

[1] When there is no difference in pitch there cannot be an interval. It is convenient, however, to regard the 1st or Unison as such.

36. The 8th and 5th, with their inversions, the 1st and 4th, are called Perfect intervals.

37. There is one peculiarity of perfect intervals by which they are easily recognised when written on a staff—namely, that the two notes which make a perfect interval are both the same kind of note—both natural, both sharp, both flat, double sharp, or double flat :—

38. There is only one exception from this. With any perfect 5th or 4th between a B and an F, the F is always of a kind one semitone higher than the B. Thus :—

Perfect 4ths.

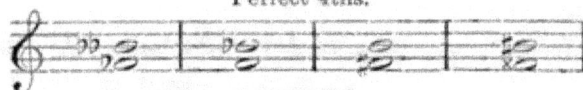

Perfect 5ths.

39. Other kinds of intervals are called Major, Minor, Augmented, and Diminished. These are best understood in connection with what are called the Major Scales.

CHAPTER IV.

INTERVALS IN CONNECTION WITH THE MAJOR SCALES.

40. The white keys of the pianoforte between any C and its octave form the Major Key of C.

41. When these keys are played ascending and descending in alphabetical order, they form the Diatonic Major Scale of C :—

42. The note that gives its name to the key is called the Tonic or Key-note; the 2nd note is called the Super-tonic; the 3rd is

called the Mediant; the 4th the Sub-dominant; the 5th the Dominant; the 6th the Sub-mediant, and the 7th the Leading Note.[1]

43. In the above example of the scale of C (sec. 41), there is a tone between each two following sounds, except the 3rd and 4th, 7th and 8th, between which there are semitones, E to F and B to C.

44. All the major scales consist of exactly the same arrangement of tones and semitones, the difference between them being only one of pitch.

45. Now, if the white keys on the pianoforte between G and its octave be written —

the arrangement of the tones and semitones is different, as there is a semitone between the 6th and 7th, and a tone between the 7th and 8th. To make this scale similar to the scale of C, ♯F must be taken instead of ♮F :—

46. The scale a perfect 5th *above* C has therefore one sharp, and the note that is thus made sharp is the leading note F. The perfect 5th above G will have its leading note in addition a ♯ — *i.e.* ♯C—and the notes will be major scale of D :—

47. Similarly, each succeeding scale, having its tonic a perfect 5th above the last, has one more sharp, and that always the 7th, or leading note.

---

[1] *Tonic*, because the key or prevailing tonality proceeds from it. *Super-tonic*, over the tonic. *Dominant*, because the harmony derived from it has a dominating or ruling influence over the key. *Mediant*, midway between tonic and dominant. *Sub-dominant*, under dominant, being the same interval, a perfect 5th, below the tonic, as the dominant is over it, and having a dominating influence subordinate to that of the dominant. *Sub-mediant*, because holding the same position under the tonic, between that and the sub-dominant, as the mediant holds over the tonic between that and the dominant. *Leading note*, because it leads the ear to expect the tonic to succeed it.

48. The order of keys with sharps is therefore said to be by perfect 5ths upwards, starting from C, and the last sharp, in a major key with sharps, is the leading note.

49. The sharps which occur in such scales are always written at the beginning of a musical piece, next after the clef, and form the Key Signature. These sharps are placed on the lines or spaces, where the notes themselves would be written :—

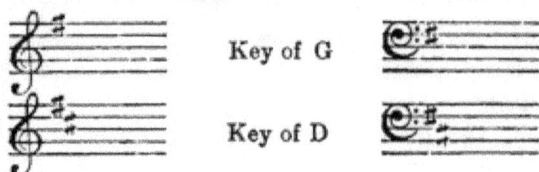

Key of G

Key of D

When a ♮ or ♭ occurs in a musical piece, which is not in the signature, it is called an Accidental.[1]

50. If the white notes between F, perfect 5th below C, and its 8th, are written—

the semitones fall between the 4th and 5th, instead of the 3rd and 4th. To remedy this ♭B is taken, the 4th of the scale or sub-dominant :—

51. The *order of major keys* with flats is therefore said to be by perfect 5ths downwards, starting from C, and the last flat in a major key with flats is the 4th or sub-dominant.

[1] Of old, the accidental applied to the same note, however long it might continue, but if it was alternated with one or more other notes, the accidental was repeated as often as the note occurred in the same bar (83). Some writers often do not repeat an accidental in a higher or lower octave, but the general rule is that the accidental applies only to the particular note against which it is placed; and unless the accidental be contradicted it applies to every repetition of the same note throughout the bar. It is often doubtful whether the first note of an ensuing bar is affected by the accidental, and for safety, therefore, it is either repeated or contradicted. An accidental is sometimes contradicted even beyond the ensuing bar of its occurrence.

52. The following shows the sharp and flat notes in seven keys above, and seven keys below, C :—

FLATS.   SHARPS.

♭C ♭G ♭D ♭A ♭E ♭B F **C** G D A E B ♯F ♯C

53. Arranged on the treble and bass staves, the signatures are as follows :[1]—

C   G   D   A   E   B   ♯F   ♯C

C   F   ♭B   ♭E   ♭A   ♭D   ♭G   ♭C

54. A perfect 4th being the inversion of a perfect 5th, the note a 4th below another has the same name as that a 5th higher, but is an octave below it. The sharps and flats have to be arranged on the staff so as not to go beyond its limits, and consequently, as is seen in the above signatures, the following sharp or flat is placed either a 5th higher or a 4th lower than the one that precedes it, as is found more convenient.

55. It is obvious that when one tonic is a 5th above or a 4th below another, the leading note of the second key is a 5th above, or a 4th below, the leading note of the first. The order in which the sharps arise is therefore also by perfect 5ths upwards, ♯F being the first.

Similarly, the order of flats is by perfect 5ths downwards, ♭B being the first.

[1] It will be observed that the signatures of two keys a chromatic semitone apart contain seven signs, whether flats or sharps.

56. Applying the above rules, let us find the signature of ♯G **major.** The leading note is the last sharp. The diatonic semitone below ♯G is the leading note, × F (F double sharp). Now the first sharp is ♯F, and the order of sharps is by perfect 5ths upwards. All the sharps therefore between ♯F and × F will form the signature required :—

♯F ♯C ♯G ♯D ♯A ♯E ♯B × F :—

57. To find the signature of ♭F **major.** The sub-dominant or perfect 4th is the last flat—*i.e.* ♭♭B. The first flat is ♭B. Between ♭B and ♭♭B are the following flats in their order, being by **perfect** 5ths downwards :—

8　　7　　6　　5　　4　　3　　2　　1
♭♭B ♭F ♭C ♭G ♭D ♭A ♭E ♭B.

The signature of ♭F major is therefore thus :--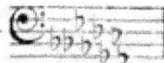

58. Return must now be made to Intervals, using, as will be shown, a complete knowledge of the major scales as a guide to determine whether a particular interval is perfect, major, minor, augmented or diminished.

59. The intervals from the tonic to any of the notes of a major scale are perfect or major. Thus, in the scale of C—

C to D is a major 2nd
C to E ,,　　,,　　3rd
C to F ,, perfect 4th
C to G ,,　　,,　　5th
C to A ,, major 6th
C to B ,,　　,,　　7th
C to C ,, perfect 8th.

60. Minor is a chromatic semitone less than **major.**

C to ♭D is a minor 2nd
C to ♭E ,,　,,　3rd
C to ♭A ,,　,,　6th
C to ♭B .. ., 7th

61. **Augmented** is a chromatic semitone higher than major or perfect.

C to ♯D is an augmented 2nd
C to ♯F   „   „   4th
C to ♯G   „   „   5th
C to ♯A   „   „   6th

62. **Diminished** is a chromatic semitone less than minor or perfect.[1]

C to ♭♭E is a diminished 3rd
C to ♭F   „   „   4th
C to ♭G   „   „   5th
C to ♭♭B   „   „   7th.[2]

63. From the above, the rules for finding the interval between two notes may be thus stated :—

(1) Take the lower note as a tonic or key-note.

(2) The intervals from that tonic to the notes in its major scale are perfect or major.

(3) When the perfect and major intervals are known, it is easy, by making them higher or lower by chromatic semitones, to find the minor, diminished, and augmented intervals.

64. Applying the above rules, let us find the interval from ♯F to D.

Taking ♯F as a tonic, we find from its major scale

that ♯F to ♯D is a major sixth, because ♯D occurs in the scale of ♯F and is the 6th note, and ♮D being a chromatic semitone lower than ♯D, the interval ♯F to D is a minor 6th (60).

65. Again, let us find the interval ♭D to B. ♭D to ♭B is a major 6th, because ♭B occurs in the major scale of ♭D, and is the 6th note. ♮B is a chromatic semitone higher than ♭B, therefore, (61), ♭D to B is an augmented 6th.[3]

[1] If the 8th or 1st were greater or less than perfect they would be called augmented and diminished 8th or 1st. These intervals are of too rare occurrence to be included in a list of intervals.

[2] Perfect intervals can thus be made both diminished and augmented. Major intervals can always be made minor and either diminished or augmented; 2nds and 6ths being augmented, 3rds and 7ths diminished.

[3] Intervals are always *reckoned* from the lower note. If exceptionally an

66. Intervals are generally reckoned as though within the octave, although they may be more than an octave apart. Thus, from C to any E above it is a 3rd : [1]—

67. We have seen (34, 35) what the number of an interval becomes when it is inverted. With regard to their quality, perfect intervals always remain perfect, major become minor, minor major, augmented diminished, and diminished augmented.

68. A 2nd inverted is a 7th, because 7 and 2 make 9 (35). Major become minor; therefore a major 2nd inverted is a minor 7th.

An augmented 6th becomes a diminished 3rd.

A perfect 5th becomes a perfect 4th.

A diminished 4th becomes an augmented 5th.

69. Perfect, major, and minor intervals are called diatonic. Augmented and diminished intervals are called chromatic.

70. Considered, however, in relation to a particular key a diatonic interval may be chromatic, and a chromatic interval diatonic. Thus F to B is an augmented 4th—a chromatic interval—but in the key of C is diatonic. C to ♭D is a diatonic interval, but in the key of C is chromatic. ♭A to ♯B, an augmented 2nd, is a chromatic interval, but in the key of C minor is diatonic.[2]

71. The following shows all the intervals, with their inversions. above E :—

Scale of E major.

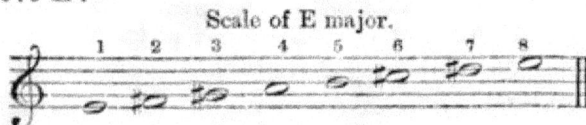

interval is required from the upper note downwards it is expressly so stated, and the application of the above rule will equally prove the correctness of the lower note when it is found.

[1] The exceptions from this are that the 2nd, 4th, and 6th, in harmony, are sometimes reckoned as the 9th, 11th, and 13th. When the exact distance is to be defined, the addition of seven to the number of any interval makes the number of the octave above such interval—3rd–10th, 5th–12th, 8th–15th.

[2] When the augmented 4th or diminished 5th are diatonic in a key, they are sometimes called tritone 4th and imperfect 5th.

Major intervals, which, when inverted, become minor :—

Perfect intervals, which, when inverted, remain perfect :—

Minor intervals, which, when inverted, become major :—

Augmented intervals, which, when inverted, become diminished :—

Diminished intervals, which, when inverted, become augmented :—

The usual method of reckoning intervals is by counting the number of semitones they contain.   Thus:—

The number of semitones in any interval added to the number of semitones in its inversion, always make the twelve which complete the octave.

71A. A Triad is a **combination** of three notes : a bass note with its third and fifth.

When the fifth **is** perfect, the Triad is called a *common chord.* When the third is major, the Triad is a *major common chord.* When the third is minor, **the** Triad is a *minor common chord.*

When the fifth is diminished, the Triad is called a *diminished Triad*. When the fifth is augmented, the Triad is called an *augmented Triad*.

In a major scale there are six common chords and one diminished Triad.

Major common chord.	Minor com. chord.	Minor com. chord.	Major com. chord.	Major com. chord.	Minor com. chord.	Diminished triad.
(1)	(2)	(3)	(4)	(5)	(6)	(7)

In a minor scale there are four common chords, two diminished Triads, and one augmented Triad.

Minor common chord.	Diminished triad.	Augmented triad.	Minor com. chord.	Major com. chord.	Major com. chord.	Diminished triad.
(1)	(2)	(3)	(4)	(5)	(6)	(7)

CHAPTER V.

MINOR KEYS AND SCALES.

72. The minor scale differs from the major in having the 3rd and 6th minor :—

C Major.

C Minor.

Augm. 2nd.

1 2 3 4 5 6 7 8

73. This is called the *Harmonic Minor Scale*, the notes being those that are used for the purposes of harmony (Def.) in the key.

74. The augmented 2nd between the 6th and 7th having a

hard effect in melody (Def.) an arbitrary alteration of the above
scale is made to secure smoothness of melody. The following
scale, in which the 6th and 7th are major in ascending and minor
in descending, is called the *Arbitrary or Melodic Minor Scale* :—

75. The key signature that is employed to denote a minor key
does not imply either of the above scales. The key signature of
a minor key is the same as that of the major key, a minor 3rd
higher. These two keys are therefore often called *relative* major
and minor.

C minor has the same signature as ♭E major—*i.e.* three
flats:— ♯F minor the same as A major—*i.e.*
three sharps :—

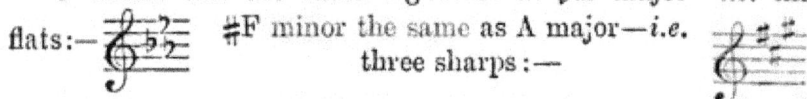

76. The leading note in the minor key has consequently an
accidental (49)—♯ or ♮—before it, in order to conform to the
harmonic minor scale ; and a musical piece is thus shown to be
in the relative minor, not the relative major : [1]—

B♭ Major.   G Minor.

77. Applying the above, here are the signatures of minor keys
with sharps, starting from A minor with none, like C major:—

Distinguishing notes.						Distinguishing notes.
♯G	Perfect 5ths upwards.	A Minor same as	C Major.			G
♯D	" "	E " " "	G "			D
♯A	" "	B " " "	D "			A
♯E	" "	F♯ " " "	A "			E
♯B	" "	C♯ " " "	E "			B

[1] All the notes in both forms of the minor scale are diatonic in spite of the

Distinguishing notes.					Distinguishing notes.
♯B	Perfect 5ths upwards.	♯C Minor same as	E Major.		B
×F	„ „	♯G „ „ „	B „		♯F
×C	„ „	♯D „ „ „	♯F „		♯C
×G	„ „	♯A „ „ „	♯C „		♯G

Here are signatures of minor keys with flats, starting as before :—

Distinguishing notes.					Distinguishing notes.
♯G	Perfect 5ths downwards.	A Minor same as	C Major.		G
♯C	„ „	D „ „ „	F „		C
♯F	„ „	G „ „ „	♭B „		F
♮B	„ „	C „ „ „	♭E „		♭B
♮E	„ „	F „ „ „	♭A „		♭E
♮A	„ „	♭B „ „ „	♭D „		♭A
♮D	·, „	♭E „ „ „	♭G „		♭D
♮G	„ „	♭A „ „ „	♭C „		♭G

78. A minor scale, starting from the same note as a major, is called the tonic minor, as opposed to the relative minor. Comparing the signatures of tonic major and minor keys, it will be seen that the minor has always three sharps less, or three flats more, than the major. As three cannot be subtracted from the one sharp in G, or two sharps in D, G loses its one sharp

and gains **two** flats, and D loses its two sharps and gains one flat, thus making a difference of three signs. C minor has three flats; C major none. A minor has none; A major three sharps.[1]

Here is a list of the signatures of minor **keys**, compared with their tonic majors :—

C major.	C minor.		G major.	G minor.
D major.	D minor.		A major.	A minor.
E major.	E minor.		B major.	B minor.
♯F major.	♯F minor.		♯C major.	♯C minor.
F major.	F minor.		♭B major.	♭B minor.
♭E major.	♭E minor.		♭A major.	♭A minor.

[1] Thus it will be observed that the last sharp in the signature of a minor key with sharps is the 2nd, the last flat in one with flats is the 6th, note of the scale.

CHAPTER VI.

CHROMATIC SCALES.

79. All the white and black keys on the pianoforte, from one key-note to its octave, form the Chromatic Scale of that key.

80. For purposes of harmony in the key each note has its true name. If the major scale and both forms of the minor be written, they will be found to contain every note but two in the chromatic scale. In each succeeding scale of the following examples the notes added by it are written large:—

Major scale of C.

Harmonic minor.

Arbitrary or Melodic minor.

Chromatic scale (Harmonic form).

81. From the above, the chromatic scale may be described as consisting of all the notes found in the major and both forms of the minor, with the addition of the minor 2nd and augmented 4th. Whence the intervals from the tonic are as follows:—

Minor and major 2nd, 3rd, 6th and 7th.

Perfect and augmented 4th and perfect 5th.

82. For convenience in reading music, the above is generally altered.

(1) The notes of the major scale are used both ascending and descending.

(2) The augmented 4th and minor 7th from the keynote are also generally used both ascending and descending.

(3) Wherever a note is required between two notes, the lower one is raised a chromatic semitone ascending, and the upper one lowered a chromatic semitone descending.

Chromatic scale of G (Melodic form).

Chromatic scale of ♭B (Melodic form).

The minims show the notes that are added to the major scale.

CHAPTER VII.

TIME.

83. In all tunes or melodies some notes are emphasised more than others. Immediately before each most strongly emphasised note a line is drawn from the top to the bottom of the staff. This is called a Bar Line, and the space between two bar lines is called a Bar.[1]

84. In the same melody each bar lasts for exactly the same time as another. It is therefore the practice to place at the beginning of a musical piece, immediately after the Key Signature, two figures to show the time of a bar. These figures are called the Time Signature.

85. One figure is placed over the other, thus, $\frac{2}{2}$. The under figure represents a note, the upper shows how many such notes there are in a bar. As there are 2 minims, 4 crotchets, 8 quavers, 16 semiquavers, or 32 demisemiquavers in a semibreve, these figures are used to indicate those notes respectively.

$\frac{2}{2}$ mean 2 minims; $\frac{3}{8}$ = 3 quavers; $\frac{4}{4}$ = 4 crotchets.

86. The time that each such note lasts is called a Division, Count, or Beat. In $\frac{2}{4}$ there are two Divisions, each continuing for as long as a crotchet :—

In playing a piece of music it is customary for a performer to count, or a conductor to beat, so many in a bar as there are divisions.[2]

87. Bars are divided into two, three, or four counts, forming

---

[1] A bar is sometimes called a measure.

[2] Each count should, however, have the *effect* of a pulse upon the hearer. In other words, time should be felt rather than counted.

Duple, Triple, or Quadruple time. Duple and quadruple are sometimes called by the one name, Common time.

88. Each division may be subdivided into any number of notes or rests of shorter length.

When more than one of any kind of notes shorter than a crotchet occur in a division, the stems of all which belong to the same division are joined together, forming one or more tails as they are quavers or notes of less value :—

89. Sometimes a count is divided into three of the notes next in value. These are called a triplet,[1] and the figure 3 is written over to indicate it :—

90. Much music is written in groups entirely like the above, when, to prevent the necessity of writing the figure 3, a new time signature is used. In the above example, where there are two divisions and three quavers in each, there is no figure to indicate the value of the one note in each count—*i.e.* a dotted crotchet—because the semibreve does not contain an equal number of dotted crotchets. The time signature is therefore expressed by figures, showing how many notes next in value—*i.e.* quavers—there are in the bar—$\frac{6}{8}$. Such a time is called Compound; those previously described, Simple.[3]

[1] Until the first third of the present century it was thought necessary that three signs, either notes or rests, should represent a triplet. At present, a crotchet and a quaver, or a quaver and a semiquaver with the figure 3, are sufficient to show that two and one make three; as a penny and a halfpenny are equal to three half-pennies. When the former principle prevailed, a dotted quaver and semiquaver were written erroneously to represent two-thirds and one-third of a crotchet and the semiquaver was to be played with the third note of the triplet. When now the same notation is employed it implies correctly that a quarter of a crotchet is shorter than a third part and is to be played after the last note of the triplet.

[2] Similarly, a crotchet may be divided into six semiquavers, the figure 6 being written over :- ; a minim into 3 crotchets or 6 quavers ; a quaver into 3 semiquavers or 6 demisemiquavers, &c.

[3] Simple, *i.e.* each count consisting of a simple note; compound, each count

91. 6, 9, and 12, when used as the upper figures of the time signature, signify 2, 3, and 4 dotted notes in a bar respectively, the dotted notes being always one degree greater than that expressed by the underneath figure :—

92. The following is a list of time signatures, those marked with an asterisk being of rarest occurrence :—

2 in a bar, or duple time.

		SIMPLE.					COMPOUND.		
2	2	2	2*	2*		6*	6	6	6	6*
2	4	8	16	32		2	4	8	16	32

3 in a bar, or triple time.

3	3	3	3*	3*		9*	9	9	9	9*
2	4	8	16	32		2	4	8	16	32

4 in a bar, or quadruple time.

4	4	4*	4*	4*		12*	12*	12	12	12
2	4	8	16	32		2	4	8	16	32

93. Four crotchets in a bar is usually expressed by this sign C.[2] Four minims in a bar, or $\frac{4}{2}$ is frequently to be found in old music written for the church or to religious words. To indicate this a line was drawn through the above sign—thus,

consisting of a dotted note (one compounded of two—as, crotchet, quaver— minim, crotchet— &c.

[1] In a composition in compound time, instead of the triplet of any division, two notes of the same kind may be taken, the division being thus made simple. The figure 2 is then placed over the notes just as triplet in simple time is indicated by the figure 3 : . The two notes may be divided into any number of smaller ones— with the figure showing their number placed over.

[2] This is intended to represent a half-circle. The circle representing perfection in ancient use expressed triple or perfect time. In opposition to this, common or imperfect time is represented by a semicircle.

₵—which nowadays implies 2 counts of a minim, and is called *Tempo alla breve*, or *a capella*.[1] The duration of a minim in the latter time is the same as that of a crotchet in $\frac{4}{4}$.

Common time, in many instances, might be marked $\frac{8}{8}$. A dot to each of the quavers induces the compound form of this time. Hence the signature $\frac{24}{16}$.

94. Wherever there is a division or beat, a stress is laid which is termed Accent. The strongest accent is always on the first of a bar.[2]

95. Good effect is often produced in a composition by placing an accent between two divisions, on what is normally an un-accented part of a bar. This effect is called Syncopation :—

[1] 'And with his stripes,' in Handel's *Messiah*, was written originally in $\frac{4}{2}$, but the bars have subsequently been cut in half, though the time signature ₵ is retained. Alla Breve means 'according to a breve,' this note, instead of the semibreve, being taken, for the occasion, as the normal note from which the shorter ones are reckoned. *Tempo a capella* obviously means 'Church time'—*i.e.* that in which compositions for church use were written.

[2] Only experience can give the required insight into this most important feature in musical composition. Composers have in some cases sanctioned the use of deceptive time signatures so that the character of the music, not the time signature, determines the accent. Much music written in $\frac{3}{4}$ time is really in $\frac{6}{4}$, two bars making one. *God Save the Queen* and an ordinary waltz are both signed $\frac{3}{4}$. The former has three accents in a bar, the latter one. In the first movement of the *Eroica Symphony* the first subject has one accent in a bar, while later on the true $\frac{3}{4}$ time is adopted. Similarly, C or $\frac{4}{4}$ should be ₵ or $\frac{2}{2}$, as in the last movement of the *Symphony in C Minor*.

[3] In old music Syncopation was frequently written thus :—

which may account for the expression 'Syncopation,' which is derived from a Greek word meaning *cutting*. The word also in grammar signifies the omission of a letter in a word; thus, musically, it may mean the omission of one accent and the substitution of another.

c 2

96. The divisions, or beats, further, are a guide as to the way in which music is written. This should always indicate the time apart from the time signature.

97. A note or rest of greater value than a division should not as a rule be used ; each division should be completed with notes or rests before the next is begun, and all the notes in a division of less value than the crotchets should be joined by the same tail or tails :—

The rule is inflexible with regard to rests except in the quadruple times in which a rest of the value of two divisions must represent the corresponding silence at the beginning or the end of a bar

Considerable variation from the rule is to be observed in the method of writing notes. In the simple times, as long as one sound continues in a bar, it may, in cases like the following, be represented by one written note. Thus :

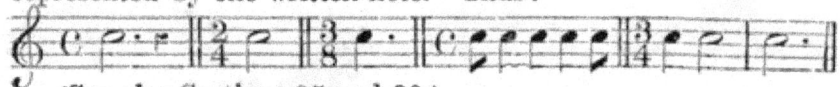

(See also Sections 95 and 98.)

In the compound times a sound lasting for two or more *whole* divisions may be represented by one written note. But if a sound lasts for one division and a portion only of the next, or for a portion of a division and the whole of the next, the rule is inflexible.

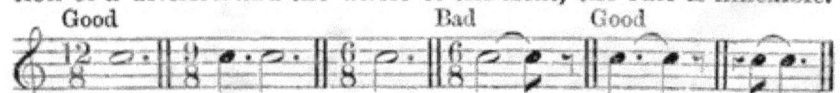

With regard to the grouping of notes; in the compound

times the rule is generally observed, but in the simple times there is some variation. In $\frac{3}{4}$ and $\frac{3}{8}$ the six quavers or semiquavers may be joined by the same tail. In C the eight quavers must be grouped in fours. Further, when a division of simple or compound time is filled by many notes of small value, they may be subdivided into groups of four or six, or these groups may be joined only by the first tail.

In music written for the voice, every fresh syllable demands a separation of the notes, but when two or more notes belong to one syllable the ordinary rules apply.

For a whole bar's silence, a semibreve rest is always used, except in alla breve time, when the whole space is filled.

Also, for several bars rest, the same sign is used with a figure placed above the staff, to show the number of silent bars :—

98. Here is a series of notes grouped according to different time signatures, with appropriate rests to fill up the odd bar wherever it is necessary :—

Attention must be directed to the last counts of bars 2 and 3 in the example in $\frac{6}{16}$ time. The last two notes of the triplet in a division of compound time may be written as one note, but the silence of these two is always shown by a rest for each.

99. In rare instances, irregular times are to be met with, such as alternate bars of $\frac{3}{4}$ and $\frac{2}{4}$ or the two joined together, making $\frac{5}{4}$.

The object of this is to ensure quaintness, or some characteristic, possibly humorous, effect.[1]

Similarly, larger notes may be divided into groups of smaller ones, containing uneven numbers of notes, otherwise than those

[1] It may be compared to a person walking with a club foot. Instances occur, however, of one such bar of $\frac{5}{4}$ time in the midst of ₵ time. The effect then is merely a prolongation of the time of one bar analogously to a *rallentando*.

described in sec. 89 and footnote; the number being shown by the corresponding figure placed over them :—

The same principle is occasionally extended to any larger number of notes.

100. Hitherto time has been described in its musical sense only, without considering the actual time occupied by each bar, as if measured by a clock. Indeed, a clock of its own has been invented for music. This is the Metronome, ascribed to Mälzel, the face of which is marked with figures from the top to the bottom, dividing the space into parts, indicated by numbers. In front is a pendulum, upon which is a movable weight which can be placed on a level with any of the numbers. The pendulum is then set free, and swings to and fro so many times in a minute as is indicated by the figure at the same level. Thus, if placed against the number 60 it will tick sixty times in a minute like a clock. The following is an example of its use as applied to a musical piece :—

Mälzel's Metronome or M.M. ♩ = 60.

meaning that each minim is to last during one tick of the pendulum, when it is rocking 60 in the minute— *i.e.* for one second of time.

CHAPTER VIII.

A SELECTION OF ITALIAN WORDS MOST COMMONLY USED IN MUSIC.

101. Loudness and softness of tone are shown by the following Italian expressions :—

Piano	. soft.
Forte	. loud.
Mezzoforte or *mf.*	. half loud.
Mezzopiano or *mp.*	. half soft.
Fortissimo or *ff.*	. loudest.
Pianissimo or *pp.*	. softest.

Fp., *forte-piano*, means that a single note is to be forte
followed by an immediate piano.

102.   *Sforzando,*   *sf.* > or ∧, forcing,
     or, *Forzato,*   *fz.*   forced,
     or, *Rinforzando*, *rf.* or *rinf.* reinforcing,

means that a single note is to be louder than the surrounding
passage. Hence less force will be used at *sf.* in a piano than at
sf. in a forte passage.

103.   *Crescendo, cresc.* or   <   , increasing.
       Decrescendo, decresc. or   > , decreasing.
       Diminuendo, dim.   diminishing.

These terms refer to the degree of loudness.

104.   *Morendo*   .   .   .   . dying away,
       Perdendosi .   .   .   . losing itself,

also refer to loudness.

105. *Ped* [1] .   .   . the sign used to indicate the lowering of
                        the pianoforte pedal nearer the right
                        foot.

    ✳   .   . sign used for raising the same pedal.

106. *Una corda* [2].   . signifies the lowering of the pedal nearer
                        the left foot.

Tre corde   .   .   . signifies that the same pedal is to be raised.

107. To show the quickness of a composition certain Italian
expressions are placed over the first staff at the left-hand corner.
The following are those in general use, ranging from the slowest
to the quickest :—

Grave   .   .   .   . grave.
Adagio   .   .   .   . slowly.
Lento   .   .   .   . slowly.
Largo   .   .   .   . largely, grandly.
Larghetto .   .   .   . diminutive of *largo*—*i.e.* a little large.
Andantino [3]   .   .   . diminutive of *andante.*

---

[1] When the right-foot pedal is used, the dampers are raised and thus the sound
is continued; utmost care must therefore be taken that this pedal be raised at every
change of harmony. The sympathetic vibration of other strings than those struck
is induced by raising the dampers, and so the use of this pedal slightly enriches
the tone. The term *senza sordini* (without dampers) is sometimes used to denote
the right-foot, or damper, pedal.

[2] When the left foot pedal is used, the hammers all shift to the right in a grand
pianoforte; one string only is affected and, consequently, softness of tone is the
result; hence, the expressions *una corda*, one string, *tre corde*, three strings. For
this latter action is substituted, in some upright pianofortes, a piece of felt which
falls on the strings and thus subdues the tone.

[3] With German writers this means less slow, with others less quick.

Andante	.	.	.	. going.
Moderato	.	.	.	. moderate.
Allegretto	.	.	.	. diminutive of *allegro.*
Allegro	.	.	.	. gay.
Vivace	.	.	.	. lively.
Presto	.	.	.	. quick.
Prestissimo	.	.	.	. augmentation of *presto—i.e.* very quick.

108. The time is hastened or slackened by the following :—

Accelerando	.	.	. accelerating ⎫ increasing the speed.
Stringendo	.	.	. drawing together ⎭
Allargando	.	.	. enlarging ⎫
Calando	.	.	. decreasing ⎪
Rallentando	.	.	. becoming slower ⎬ decreasing the speed.
Ritenuto, riten., rit.	.	. holding back the time ⎪
Ritardando, ritard., rit.	.	. retarding the time ⎭

À Tempo	.	.	·⎧ all used to show that the first time is to
Tempo primo or *Tempo*	.	·⎨ be resumed after it has been quickened
Come prima	.	.	·⎩ or retarded.

À piacere	.	.	·⎫ at pleasure (as regards the time).
Ad libitum	.	.	·⎭

L'istesso tempo . . . the same time—*i.e.* as the preceding time, though a difference of notation may imply a difference of speed. Often employed to denote a change from compound to simple time, or *vice versâ.*

109. The following are some of the expressions used to indicate the manner of performance :—

Affettuoso, or *Affettuosamente*	affectionately, or with feeling.
Agitato	.	. . . agitated.
Amoroso	.	. . . lovingly.
Animato, Animando, Con anima	. ⎫ animated, animating, with soul. ⎭
Appassionato, Con passione	passionate, with passion.
Brillante	.	. . . brilliant.
Cantabile	.	. . . in a singing style.
Col canto [1]	.	. . with the singing part.
Colla parte [1]	.	. . with the solo part.
Colla voce [1]	.	. . with the voice part.
Commodo	.	. . . easy, without haste.
Con brio	.	. . . with spirit and full tone.

[1] These have regard to the freedom of time employed by the principal performer.

Con energia	.	.	with energy.
√ Con forza	.	.	with force.
Con fuoco	.	.	with fire.
↘ Con moto	.	.	with animated movement.
Con spirito	.	.	with spirit.
Con tenerezza	.	.	with tenderness.
↘ Delicatamente	.	.	delicately.
√ Dolce	.	.	with softness and delicacy.
Dolente	.	.	in a plaintive style.
Espressivo, Con espressione	.	expressive, with expression.
Grazioso, Con grazia	.	.	graceful, with grace.
Legato (122)	.	.	bound or smooth.
Leggiero[1]	.	.	light.
↖ Lusingando	.	.	caressing.
Maestoso, Con maestà	.	majestic, with majesty.
Marcato	.	.	marked, marking.
↘ Marziale, Alla marcia	.	martial, like a march.
↘ Mesto, Con dolore	.	sadly.
Mezza voce	.	.	with half voice—i.e. moderate power.
↘ Non tanto	.	.	not so much.
Non troppo	.	.	not too much.
↘ Parlante	.	.	in a style of recitation.
Pesante	.	.	heavy.
Pomposo	.	.	pompous.
Recitativo	.	.	recitative—i.e. the delivery of the words as in a recitation, to musical phrases with great freedom as to time.
Risoluto	.	.	resolute.
Scherzando	.	.	playing (playful).
Smorzando	.	.	fading away.
↘ Soave	.	.	delicately, gently.
Solo	.	.	part to be performed by one person.
Sostenuto	.	.	sustained.
↩ Sotto voce	.	.	under the voice—i.e. subdued tone.
Staccato (123)	.	.	detached.
√ Tempo giusto	.	.	at a moderate pace.
√ Tempo ordinario	.	.	at ordinary marching pace.
Tenuto	.	.	held.
Tranquillo	.	.	tranquil.
Tutti	.	.	what is to be performed by a full band or chorus.
Vivo	.	.	lively.

[1] The affix mente, like the syllable ly in English, changes a word into an adverb; as Leggieramente, lightly.

110. The following are used in conjunction with the above : —

A or *ad*	.	at.
At	.	to the.
Assai	.	very.
Ben	.	well.
Come	.	as.
Con	.	with.
Da	.	from.
Dal	.	from the.
Di	.	of.
Ed or *E*	.	and.
Ma	.	but.
Meno	.	less, as *meno mosso.*
Molto, Di molto	.	much.
Mosso	.	moved (as to speed).
Più	.	more, as *più allegro.*
Poco a poco	.	little by little.
Poi	.	then.
Quasi	.	as though.
Sempre	.	always.
Senza	.	without.
Simile	.	like—*i.e.* as before.
Un poco	.	a little.

CHAPTER IX.

ABBREVIATIONS AND OTHER SIGNS.

111. At the end of a composition two thick bar lines are drawn across the staff. These are called a Double bar. A double bar also occurs in the course of a movement to show the end of some separate division : —

112. A double bar with two or four dots placed in the spaces on either side is called a Repeat, and signifies that the portion of the music on the side of the double bar at which the dots are placed is to be performed twice.

113. For the one bar or more before a repeat new matter is often substituted, which is written after the double bar. Over

the former is placed a bracket, with the words *First time*, or *Prima volta*, signifying that it is to be played the first time only ; over the latter is written *Second time*, or *Seconda volta*, signifying that it is to be played instead of the other, after the repeat :—

114. The expression *Da capo* signifies that the music is to be repeated from the beginning, and is most usually applied to movements like the Minuet and Trio; *Minuetto da capo*, written at the end of the Trio, showing that the Minuet is to be repeated, but not the Trio (119).

115. When the repeat is not to be from the beginning, the words *Dal segno* (from the sign) are used, directing to this sign 𝄋 at the point whence the repeat is to be made, and the words *Al segno* (to the sign) direct to the same mark at the point where the repetition is to end.

116. If the music of one bar is repeated in the next, this sign (——) may be used in the second bar to save writing out the notes twice :—

Or one oblique stroke may be used as often as a group of quavers in any division of a bar is to be repeated, two strokes being used for a repetition of semiquavers, three for one of demisemiquavers, &c.

The word *Bis* (twice) under a bracket implies that the passage over which it is placed is to be performed twice.

117. A longer note may be divided into iterations of the

same note by drawing through the stem one or more strokes; one stroke signifying iterations of the value of a quaver; two strokes, iterations of semiquavers; three, iterations of demisemiquavers, and so on. In the case of notes with one or more hooks, each hook counts for a stroke. The figure 3 or 6, with a dot after a note, implies that triplets or sextolets of the shorter notes are to fill up the time of the longer note :—

118. When two minims are joined by a quaver, semiquaver, or demisemiquaver tail, there are to be as many alternations of the two notes with quavers, semiquavers, or demisemiquavers as will fill up the time of one of the written notes :—

Trem., *Tremolo*, or *Tremolando* (trembling), signifies that there are to be as many alternations or iterations as possible in the time.

119. When sound or silence is to be indefinitely prolonged, irrespective of time, this sign (⌢), called the Pause, is placed over the note or the rest. The letters G. P. (*Grosse or General Pause*) the words *Lunga pausa*, or *Lunga*, have a similar significance. Either a pause over the double bar (sometimes the final note), or else the word *Fine* (finish), is often used to show where the music is to finish after the repeat or *Da capo* (114).

120. To avoid the use of an inconvenient number of leger lines, *8va*, followed by a line of dots over the staff, means that the passage is to be played *an octave higher* so far as the dots

continue. *Ottava bassa,* more rarely *Ottara sotto,* under the staff, means that the passage is to be played an octave lower. The word *Loco* (place) is sometimes used to show where the real pitch of the notes is to be resumed.[1]

121. *Arpeggio* or *Arpeggiando,* written over a chord, signifies that the notes are not to be played together, but successively, as on a harp. The same result is to be obtained by these signs ⎱ (:—

Written.

Played.

122. Instead of the general expression *Legato,* a sign called a Slur is used ⌒, to show that all the notes it embraces are to be played smoothly one after the other without any break in the continuity of the sound :—

When but two notes are slurred, the first should be pressed and the second given with lightness :—

When the same note is written twice, the slur that joins the two is called a Tie or Bind, and then the second is to be held on as if the two were one continued sound. Some call the Slur a Bind (4).

123. Instead of the general expression *Staccato,* a dot or a dash under or over a note signifies that the sound is to be disconnected from that which follows :[2]—

---

[1] The expression *ottava* is rarely seen in the bass staff, the effect being obtained by the insertion of the C or G clefs. Similarly, *ottava bassa* is never seen in the treble staff, the effect being obtained by the insertion of the F clef.

[2] The explanation of the difference between the dot and dash, and the combi-

124. The *Appoggiatura* (leaning note) was written in small character. It is played with pressure, always has the value of the note written, and takes so much time from the following note. It is rarely at a greater distance than a second above or below the next note :[1]—

Written.　　　　　　　　　　　　Played.

125. The *Acciaccatura* (crushing note) is to be played as quickly as possible, without taking any appreciable time from the succeeding note. It is written like a quaver *appoggiatura*, but with a stroke through the stem and tail :—

Played.

126. Groups of two or more notes written small often precede long notes, and, with rare exceptions, they are to be played before the division of a bar that contains the accented note :—

127. The Shake, or Trill (*tr*) is the alternation of a written note and the note above it as rapidly as possible. In modern music two small notes are written on the staff, as in the example below, to form a finish to the shake. In music of earlier date this is never found, and was never intended to be played.[2]

nation of the slur with either, belongs to the teaching of particular instruments. In no case is the time of notes so marked to be shortened in relation to that of the whole bar.

[1] The use by modern composers of a small note for the *appoggiatura* is now obsolete. It being a note foreign to the harmony, the device was originally employed when unprepared discords, such as the *appoggiatura*, were considered heterodox ; as if the heinousness of the offence were palliated by making the discord appear insignificant alongside its fellow notes.

[2] Some persons define the shake as a series of *appoggiaturas*, over the written note, the shake to commence with the upper note. Beethoven, and others who employ this latter interpretation, write an *acciaccatura* before the note bearing the shake when they mean that, exceptionally, such upper note is to be played first.

A ♯, ♭, or ♮ over a shake shows that the upper note is to be inflected accordingly :—

128. The Mordent (𝈈) indicates that the written note and the note above it are to be played as rapidly as possible, returning to the written note :—

129. The Inverted Mordent is written thus ✦, and indicates that the written note and the note below it are to be played as rapidly as possible.

130. The Turn or *Gruppetto* (∿) consists of the note above that over which the turn is marked, followed by the written note, the note below, and then the written note again. A ♯, ♭, or ♮ written over or under the turn shows that the note over or under the written note is to be inflected accordingly. When the ornament is marked over a plain note, the four notes are of equal length, and are to be played more or less quickly, according to the time of the movement :—

When placed over a dotted note, the turn consists of the first three notes, and, instead of the fourth, a note the length of the dot is played :—

131. The Inverted Turn (⌇ or ⌇) consists of the note below that on which the turn is marked, followed by the written note, the note above, and then the written note again :—

The various modifications of the above ornamentations require explanation from teachers of particular instruments, and are too elaborate to come under the title *Elements of Music.*

D

INDEX.

Spottiswoode & Co. Printers, New-street Square, London.

SIX LECTURES

ON

MUSICAL HARMONY

DELIVERED AT THE ROYAL INSTITUTION OF GREAT BRITAIN

By Sir G. A. MACFARREN.

THE purpose of this work is to offer to the musical laity an account of the principles of harmonic combination which may help insight into the application of these in composition, and thus to a keener perception of beauty in music than can arise through the ear alone, unaided by the understanding. Though it may assist the more serious student, its design is, by copious illustration of the rules on which the art rests, to make these obvious even to readers who, with love for the subject, have not time or inclination for its elaborate pursuit. The lectures refer to a prevailing mis-apprehension as to the relationship between the mediæval ecclesiastical system and that of the classic Greeks, and to the inaptitude of the former for standard use in the Church of England. They describe the distinctions between what may be called archaic art in music and the style whose morning stars were PURCELL, HANDEL, and BACH, and whose broadest daylight is the expansion of their lustre and its manifold reflexion, rather than the revelation of a new source of radiance. These two styles were first separated and defined by ALFRED DAY, and it is his original, perspicuous, and comprehensive views that are set forth by the Author, who owned him as a friend and as a guide. The ancient, strict or contrapuntal style is shewn to .be arbitrary and artificial; the modern, free or massive, to be impulsive and natural. The two are confounded by many meritorious musicians; to distinguish them may lead to the clearer production as well as comprehension of music.

LONGMANS, GREEN, & CO. 39 Paternoster Row, London
New York and Bombay.

www.ingramcontent.com/pod-product-compliance
Lightning Source LLC
Chambersburg PA
CBHW022041080426
42733CB00007B/924